THE BOOK OF
ALEXANDER SARCOPHAGUS

THE BOOK OF
ALEXANDER SARCOPHAGUS

Dr. Alpay Pasinli

A TURİZM YAYINLARI

JACKET AND COVER PICTURE
Alexander the Great. Detail from long side A

Editors
Margaret Oliphant & Fatih Cimok

First printing 1997
Second printing 2000

Publishers
A Turizm Yayınları Ltd. Şti.
Şifa Hamamı Sokak 18, Sultanahmet 34400, İstanbul
Tel: (0212) 517 44 72 - 517 44 74 - 516 24 97; Fax: 516 41 65
e-mail: aturizm @ superonline.com

CONTENTS

INTRODUCTION

The Alexander Sarcophagus has been a major attraction of the İstanbul Archaeological Museum ever since it was founded in the late nineteenth century. Although named after Alexander the Great, the sarcophagus was not his, but was probably that of Abdalonymos, the last king of Sidon (Saida).

Abdalonymos owed his throne to Alexander and the latter's close friend and general, Hephaistion. The subject matter of the reliefs decorating the sarcophagus suggests that Abdalonymos was here commemorating his benefactors; the sarcophagus thus takes its name, not from the ruler who commissioned it, but from its iconography.

Alexander III, better known as 'the Great' (336-323 BC) was the son of Philip II of Macedon and Olympia, who was famous for her ambition and interest in politics. The young Alexander was educated by the best tutors of his time, including Aristotle.

Following his father's assassination, Alexander succeeded him, consolidated his position in Greece and then embarked on his eastern expedition. Crossing the Dardanelles with some forty thousand soldiers, he defeated the Persians at Granicus (334 BC) and advanced through Anatolia. In the course of this march, he cut the Gordion knot.

After his victory over a large force of Persians under Darius III at Issos (333 BC), he took control of Phoenicia, Palestine and Egypt. His final defeat of Darius at Gaugamela near the upper Tigris (331 BC) opened the gates of Persia. His bright career was stained by the burning of Persepolis, though whether, as has been claimed, this was on his orders or by accident, is not known.

In 327 BC he marched east and captured the north of India, as far as the Beas and lower Indus. His troops now refused to go any further and he returned to Babylon, having covered some twenty thousand kilometres. Here, at the age of 33, he died suddenly of fever in 323 BC.

From the surviving literary evidence about the sarcophagus made for Alexander, it is clear that monument had no similarity with the one which is the subject of this volume. After he died Alexander's friends and generals are said to have made for their king a hammered gold sarcophagus in the form of his embalmed body. The first-century-BC writer Diodorus Siculus relates that *First they fashioned a plate of beaten gold molded to the form of the body. Above it was placed a golden lid... Then they were shown the bier intended to transport the remains, its top adorned with mother-of-pearl studded with precious stones. The peristyle was embellished with columns of the Ionian order... In all, sixty-four mules were required to pull it.* The sarcophagus was covered with a purple cloth on which the arms of Alexander: helmet, swordbelt, shields and greaves and ceremonial cuirass — the one used in the battle having been too worn — were put.

The funeral cortège first took the North-Syrian route to travel to Macedon. However, after reaching the coast it turned south and following the coastal route, travelled to Memphis in Egypt (for a pharaoh's burial), and afterwards to Alexandria where the sarcophagus became the major sight of the city while the tomb was being completed. The change in the plan appears to have been the idea of his general, Ptolemy, who was then the satrap of Egypt. This is where the story of the actual sarcophagus of Alexander ends.

ROYAL NECROPOLIS OF SIDON

The group of twenty-two sarcophagi which were discovered in 1887 at Sidon are among the most important works of classical archaeology. The necropolis was discovered accidentally by a villager while he was trying to dig a well. When news of the discovery reached İstanbul, Osman Hamdi Bey, who was then the director of the Ottoman Imperial Museum (today's İstanbul Archaeological Museum), went to Lebanon and supervised the excavations personally.

The sarcophagi were placed in two groups of underground burial chambers both of which were insulated against humidity and water seepage and around a rectangular well of about 10 m depth. The first group consisted of seven rooms. Apart from a cavity which hid an Egyptian anthropoid sarcophagus, all of the rooms had been robbed at an unknown date. The second underground chamber was intact. After the excavations, the finds were carried to İstanbul by boat. A few years later they were placed in the museum which was built for their presentation and are still on display in their original positions. As with the Alexander Sarcophagus they are named after the subject of their reliefs and include the Sarcophagus of Mourning Women, the Satrap Sarcophagus, the Lycian Sarcophagus and the Tabnit Sarcophagus.

The result of later research suggests that these sarcophagi belonged to a successive group of kings who ruled in Sidon between the middle of the fifth and the last part of the fourth centuries BC. They were put into the burial vaults in their order of succession, and the Alexander Sarcophagus was probably the last to be sculpted and placed in the burial chamber.

THE ALEXANDER SARCOPHAGUS

The Alexander Sarcophagus is one of the most important work of Hellenistic relief sculpture[1] in existence. Made of Pentelic[2] marble and exquisitely carved in very high relief, it has survived in almost pristine condition, with only a small amount of damage. This was perhaps the work of tomb robbers, who removed the metal attachments that provided the detail for weapons, reins, bridles and other furnishings.

The figures, their costumes and other details were also painted, which would have added further depth and richness to the work. As much of this survives, the sarcophagus is also important as evidence for the effect of colour on ancient sculpture.

It is thought that some damage also occurred when the sarcophagus was transported from the workshop to the burial chamber. Given the risks of transporting such a delicate but heavy work of art over long distances, it seems likely that it was produced at Sidon. Scholars think that it was commissioned by and made for Abdalonymos, the last king of the city. On the order of Alexander, he was appointed to this position by Hephaistion in 332 BC.

The subject matter of the reliefs and external historical evidence date it firmly to the late fourth century BC; it was probably designed and executed some time between 325 and 311, and completed shortly after Abdalonymos's death in 312 BC. The commissioning of a sarcophagus some time before death, by the person for whom it was intended, was not unusual in antiquity.

The chest of the sarcophagus has six panels carved in high relief. One of each of the longer and shorter panels are battle scenes; the other two are of hunting. Those on the pediments of the lid are scenes of combat. Although all of the scenes are worked in separate panels with frames, they constitute a unity. To facilitate the tracing of reliefs and their description, they are desig-

[1] The other being the Great Altar of Pergamum (now in Berlin)

[2] From Mt Pentelikon near Athens

nated long side A, long side B, short side A, pediment A, short side B and pediment B.

These reliefs of Greeks and Orientals, adversaries in battle and companions at hunting, not only decorate the monument and commemorate events of supreme importance in the life of Abdalonymos they relate also to kingship, to the duties and pleasures of kings, in war and at peace, to their relationships with each other, and in particular, to that between Abdalonymos and Alexander.

After defeating Darius III (336-330 BC) at Issos in 333 BC, Alexander advanced along the coast of the Mediterranean, where most of the Phoenician cities welcomed him. These city states had earlier been vassals of Assyria, then of Babylonia and since the mid-sixth century, part of the Achaemenid Persian Empire.

They were governed by local Semitic Canaanite dynasties, who seem to have adopted the rich and luxurious Persian way of life. Iron ores and timber of the mountains and murex of the Mediterranean, which produced valuable purple dye, were among the important products of the region. The Phoenicians had long been skilled traders and mariners, and from the coastal cities such as Byblos, Tyre and Sidon, copper from Cyprus and other merchandise reached the hinterland. By the mid-fourth century, many of the wealthy cosmopolitan people of this region had adopted Persian fashions of dress and pursuits.

Except at Tyre, Alexander met with no resistance from the Phoenicians and the people of Sidon actually opened the gates of their prosperous city to the Greeks. Discontented with their pro-Persian ruler, they asked Alexander to appoint a new king. Not having enough time to do this himself, the task was given to Hephaistion, who chose Abdalonymos.

Distantly related to the Sidonian royal house, the new king, whose name in Persian means 'servant of god', had been living a modest life in the countryside, keeping himself busy growing flowers. If the story has any real basis, Abdalonymos rapidly adjusted to his new state, for it was he who is thought to have commissioned this splendid monument with reliefs of himself and his benefactors.

Abdalonymos is thought to be represented in three of the reliefs; like his companions, he wears Persian dress, as was then customary amongst the Phoenician elite. Although Alexander, Hephaistion or others of high rank are clearly defined, Greeks and Macedonians are not however distinguished from each other by their uniforms, arms or physiognomy. Both are therefore referred to as 'Greek'.

As a general rule, the Greeks in the reliefs wear clothes of one colour. Some wear only the *chlamys*, whilst most have short tunics with sleeves and *chlamyses* fastened at the right shoulder.[3] The tunic is often girded twice, with the lower belt concealed and the upper belt — often displayed and made of leather with a metal fitting — worn on the overpiece falling below the waist. They are either bare-footed or wear sandals with anklestraps, which were indicated by brushwork.

The costume of the Persians is more uniform, but more colourful and conforms to the Persian tradition that banned display of men's bodies except for the face and fingertips. It consists of loose trousers, *anaxyrides*, with ends tucked into the shoes, a long-sleeved tunic belted at the waist and *kandys*, namely a cloak with long sleeves, lined with a different colour and flowing freely at the back; they also wear head coverings held by ribbons tied round the head, and shoes. The Persians wear no armour; some carry bows and axes and their shields are either round or of the Greek *pelta*[4] type.

Some of the Greeks have rigid metal cuirasses and their helmets are of the conical Phrygian or the Boeotian type, which Alexander introduced because it protected the neck and gave better all round vision. Their shields are round, sometimes decorated on one side, and they are armed with swords or lances.

Although Alexander's army was composed of both Macedonian soldiers and Greek auxiliaries, they were not on friendly terms. Whilst the former regarded the latter as degenerate and without character, the Greeks thought of the Macedonians as half-civilized barbarians. Nevertheless, this was the army with which Alexander defeated the Persians and acquired everlasting fame.

[3] The exceptions to the general information given here are indicated in the description of relief panels.

[4] A small crescent-shaped shield

LONG SIDE A

This vigorous frieze captures the tumult of the final stage of a battle, with the Greek victory nearly secured. In the chaos, Persians lie dead or mortally wounded, their cavalry almost routed. At each end and in the centre, is a mounted figure on a rearing charger, perfectly establishing the balance of this composition. Between them are groups of soldiers engaged in a series of individual combats. In all, eighteen figures have been accommodated in this confined space, creating a dramatic representation of a battle, thought to be that of Issos. It was Alexander's victory here, that shortly afterwards, gave to Abdalonymos the throne of Sidon.

On the far left of the composition Alexander is mounted and charging at a Persian soldier. His elaborate headgear, the pelt of the Nemean lion's head — symbol of Heracles from whom he claimed descent, helps to distinguish him. The coins issued at Sidon's mint also depict him as the young Heracles wearing this traditional trophy. In addition, next to his ear is a ram's horn, the symbol of the Egyptian god Ammon, whom he adopted as his father after visiting the oracle of Siwa in the Libyan desert. Here he was hailed as 'Son of Ammon', or in Greek terms 'Son of Zeus'.[5] The tradition of deification he began was to be repeated by the kings who inherited his empire and ultimately, in a more clearly prescribed formula, by Roman emperors. Unlike other Greek soldiers who are draped in short-sleeved tunics, he wears a long-sleeved tunic like that of the Persian soldiers. Above the waist, his garment is held by a belt with a buckle. His right foot is missing.

Alexander is represented in a naturalistic manner with short hair. He is known to have rarely worn a cuirass. His raised right arm is in the act of hurling a spear which must have been metal. His horse which has received an arrow in its shoulder, is trampling on the body of a Persian. Above the hoof the animal's right leg shows ancient restoration. Originally, the eyes, lips, hair and shoes of Alexander were painted in a red brown. The lion's pelt adorning his head was in yellow with brown eyes. His tunic was in purple-blue and the mantle burgundy. The harness, muzzle and contour lines of his horse's eyes were red brown, its breast ochre yellow with touches of red brown. The arrow buried in its breast, and the bit and bridle were metal. The purpose of the hole is not known. The animal had a yellow saddle with a fringed border in blue. Its reins and girth were red brown; its breast collar was ochre yellow with touches of red brown.

The Persian soldier lying under the hooves of Alexander's horse had a blue tunic with a red belt. His shoes were red brown.

[5] The cult of Ammon is said to have reached Greece where the god was portrayed as Zeus with curling ram's horns on his head as early as the seventh century BC.

The horse of the Persian soldier whom Alexander is about to strike, is rendered in profile and has fallen on to its forelegs towards the right. Its skin was of reddish tone. The forelock is ribboned. Originally its saddle was shown with double coloured border. Its rider is dressed in the typical Persian manner: a long-sleeved tunic, which was light burgundy, girded with a red brown belt, purple anaxyrides decorated with a yellow band, a yellow tiara and yellow brown shoes. The kandys was ochre brown with lining indicated in brown and sleeves in sky-blue ending in purple at the wrist. Its terrified rider while disengaging himself from the animal by moving his left leg to the other side, is trying to defend himself against Alexander, with his sword raised in his right hand. The hole in the middle of his belt indicates the existence of a metal belt buckle. This soldier and his falling horse were possibly inspired by a scene thought to represent the battle of Issos or Gaugamela painted by Philoxenus of Eretria at the time that the sarcophagus was executed. The animal had a metal bit and bridle.

The neighbouring representation is of a Persian soldier engaged in combat with a Greek commander. The Persian soldier has lost his weapons — his broken lance in the background was ochre — and has raised his hands helplessly in an instinctive gesture of protection. His left wrist and hand are missing. The fingers of his other hand are mutilated. His hair, lips, eye-brows and eye contours and irises were red brown with the pupils emphasized in darker tone. He wore a reddish tunic with sleeves in bright red. His anaxyrides was probably red, and shoes yellow. The band which holds his ochre brown tiara is clearly indicated around his head.

The armoured Greek soldier covering himself with his shield has raised his sword, thought to have been of marble, against his enemy. Over a bright red inner tunic he wears rigid metal armour in red with leather strip protectors on his upper arms and attached to his belt forming a sort of kilt protecting his thighs. He does not wear a chlamys. In reality, his greaves, Phrygian helmet, cuirass and waist belt would have been bronze. His sleeves lined with red material to prevent chafing. The garters were shown in red. His blue helmet bore a white spiral around the casque, which may have been the sign of his rank. The side plumes of his casque of which one was shown were metal. It is known that Alexander replaced this type of helmet with the Boeotian type, worn by the other two Greek horsemen on this side of the chest, which gave more protection to the face and shoulders. His oblique shoulder belt was indicated in blue. His scabbard was ochre and white. His left leg stands heedlessly on the fallen body of a Persian.

Behind the Greek soldier and in the third plane, a Persian soldier with a red moustache aims an arrow at Alexander. The cord of his bow was shown in red brown. A blue spot behind the helmet of the Greek soldier is thought to have belonged to an arrowhead.

In the foreground, a Persian soldier has bent one knee to the ground and raised his shield to protect himself. His arm, weaponless, is extended forward and his open hand rests on the flank of enemy's horse. He wears a yellow tiara with touches of red, a yellowish tunic, anaxyrides with a yellow right leg and the other purple. His shoes were painted in red brown with the soles indicated in darker tones. The interior of his shield was burgundy with an ochre yellow rim, banded in blue. The armgrip was indicated in blue.

A mounted Greek trying to manage his horse with his left hand, has turned three-quarters backwards and is about to strike a Persian soldier. The Greek wears a Boeotian helmet. Originally, his saddle was rendered in red with a border of white dots and decorated with figures of the same colour with contours in blue. The design consisted probably of a lion and two winged griffons whose bodies were partly covered with the right hand of the kneeling Persian soldier. The saddle cloth was an animal skin with a thick red fringe. The girth was red and breast collar blue with a border in ochre yellow and red brown. It has been claimed that the mounted Greek represented Alexander's general, Parmenion, who had also served his father, Philip II. However, he would have been seventy years old by this date and the figure in the relief is too young to be him. In addition, Parmenion was accused of conspiracy against Alexander and was killed in 330 BC. Abdalonymos is unlikely to have included a traitor on the reliefs of his sarcophagus.

Beneath the horse the prostrate body of a Persian — his yellow tiara fallen from his head — is partly covered by his red-painted pelta which had a yellow and white rim and bore a motif in yellow at its centre.

In the foreground, a Persian soldier who is kneeling on the ground is aiming an arrow at a mounted Greek commander on the right of the battle scene. Originally, his bow was metal. His costume was decorated with various colours of different designs. It is known that Persian soldiers could wear any colour or decoration.

In the background on the second plane a mounted and armed Persian is charging a Greek with his sword. He is dressed in the typical Persian manner. His burgundy anaxyrides had a border along its seam on the right leg. The eyes of his horse were blue, reins red brown, breast collar red between ochre yellow above and red brown below. His saddle was shown in blue paint and probably bore an animal figure of the same colour with contours in white.

The Greek soldier's cloak has fallen from his shoulders and left his body naked and he is bareheaded. His hair, eyes and lips bear traces of red brown. With his left hand he grasps the lower bridle of his adversary's horse and raises his sword with the other hand. He is thought to be an infantryman or a dismounted cavalryman. His cloak bears traces of purple.

The combat shows a Persian who has raised his pelta to protect himself and his dead friend from the mounted Greek on the right. The tunic of the Persian bears traces of blue. His belt was ochre yellow, the anaxyrides probably purple. The right arm of his long-sleeved.tunic shows traces of red brown. The interior of his shield was painted in burgundy. The head has not survived. The fingers of his comrade's left hand are also missing. The latter falls lifeless from his horse. His tunic shows traces of yellow and red brown paint. His anaxyrides was violet; the shoe was probably blue, with its sole in red brown. The saddle of the animal was blue, with a bright red border decorated with foliage motif in white and a large fringe in blue. Its girth was red, breast collar yellow and red brown. The wounds on its chest and neck were bleeding. Under the horses' hooves are the corpses of a Greek who has fallen on his round shield and a Persian. The Greek's hair was ochre yellow. The wound on his chest and upper left arm were soaked in blood, shown in red. The Persian mouth is open and his lifeless left arm rests on his chest. A red shield with ochre yellow border and a lance in ochre brown were painted on the background surface.

25

The Greek commander, with whom the representation on this face terminates, is charging at the Persian with a lance in his raised right hand, which was shown in ochre brown. He wears a long-sleeved tunic in purple with its wrist in yellow, and a purple chlamys. The umber strip below the tunic on his thigh may indicate the existence of an inner tunic. A panther-skin shabrack with brown speckles was placed over the saddle cloth. The traces of an animal's paw marks have survived on his horse. The bridle, unlike the bit, was not metal but shown in paint.

This is an unusual figure of an old soldier, his face hidden in the shade of the visor of his plain bronze Boeotian helmet. His expression radiates brutal energy. He has received a metal arrow below his left knee which is bleeding. His helmet has a white or silver wreath which was probably the insignia of his rank in the army. Alexander was also known to have given gold crowns to the soldiers who had distinguished themselves in battle. The figure also wears bracelets as badges of his rank, originally a Persian tradition. The handle and scabbard of his straight stabbing sword, slung on his left side, were brown. His coat of mail was in yellow. He is thought to represent Perdiccas, one of Alexander's generals and his second-in-command.

The representation of battle was the most popular way of expressing the courage of a ruler and an indispensable part of ancient royal iconography. The tradition went back to ancient Mesopotamian rulers and pharaohs of Egypt. In such compositions the royal figure is often shown in the act of killing an enemy or towering over the dead enemy. Scholars believe that the scene on this side represents the battle of Issos between the forces of Alexander and the Achaemenid king, Darius III. In November 333 BC the armies met on ground unfavourable to the Persian cavalry, where the Amanus Mts lie closest to the Mediterranean, near the modern town of Dörtyol in Turkey. The topography of the area may have changed since antiquity and scholars are not in agreement on the exact spot where the battle was fought.

LONG SIDE B

Less crowded than the other side and less vital, this composition is oriented towards the centre, where Abdalonymos, accompanied by Alexander, is shown hunting a lion. Here too, the sculptor(s) has (have) used three mounted figures, intended to establish a balance, though not entirely successfully.

In ancient tradition the royal hunt was one of the ways of displaying the bravery of ruler. Various finds from Mesopotamia and Egypt show kings engaged in hunting elephants, lions and other animals, whether or not they actually did. In Mesopotamian iconography the epic hero Gilgamesh was often represented slaying a lion. Traditionally regarded as a shepherd protecting his people, an Assyrian ruler had a duty to defend his subjects. In this context they ritually hunted lion and other animals. A series of reliefs shows them participating in elaborate lion hunts. This tradition was adopted by Achaemenid and other Near Eastern rulers. It was one of the most important sports of the Oriental monarchs and Abdalonymos is said to have taken Alexander to the animal parks of old Sidon for hunting. Alexander is also known to have hunted elephants in India. The hunting motif

reached Greece even before the conquest of Persia by Alexander and continued to be used in the Hellenistic period. In his *Anabasis* Xenophon relates that on their way to Persia (*c.* 401 BC), the younger Cyrus and his forces stopped at Celaenae in Phrygia, where the Persian prince hunted in a large park full of wild animals. The Persian satrap Pharnabazus is also said to have had a similar park in his capital at Daskylaion (Ergili, Manyas).

The representation begins with an Oriental in Persian dress, who is in the act of releasing an arrow. His metal bow has not survived. His hair, lips and eye contours were in red brown. His tiara was purple with a red flap at the back. His tunic and anaxyrides were purple and kandys dark blue. The sleeves of the latter were purple. His shoes were brown.

In front of him a naked Greek rushes to the struggle. His *ephaptis*, or military 'wrap-around' cloak used by the heavy infantry, is rolled around his left arm. This garment consisted of a long narrow rectangular piece of cloth which was normally thrown over the left shoulder, but in case of necessity wrapped round the arm to function as a shield during hunting or a fight. The cloth was bright red. The carving of his fingers indicates that he was armed with a metal lance in his left hand and a hunting axe in the other. This figure, almost completely detached from the surface of the chest, is one of the most magnificent examples of Greek art of this period. Unfortunately the head has not survived. Alongside him a greyhound bounds towards the hunt. Its tail bears traces of yellow and on its collar and the ears and eyes brown has been distinguished.

The next figure, of a Greek commander, gallops to assist the horseman in front of him. His head has indentations for attaching a royal diadem. Thus, although his physiognomy and dress do not differ from the other Greeks on the sarcophagus, he is thought to represent Alexander. He has discarded his armour for the hunt and was probably armed with a short metal hunting spear. His hair, lips and eyes were painted in red brown but the pupils were darker. His tunic was purple and chlamys ochre yellow, with its lower border in purple. The faint brown marking fringe on his thigh, along the border of the long-sleeved tunic, was probably an inner tunic. His red brown shoes had yellow soles.

The breast collar of his horse was red brown and brown and its saddle was probably in ochre yellow. The leather strap which held its tail was unfastened and flowing and was shown in brown on the background. Beneath his mount, a greyhound leaps towards the lion.

Although Alexander is thought to have participated in actual lion hunts, this representation is also an allusion to the slaying of the Nemean lion by Heracles, also a son of Zeus. Alexander is known to have taken part in a hunt staged in the Persian royal park at Sidon, which must have been a game preserve, known as *pairidaeza* or *paraidesos*[1] in Persian, an enclosed garden.

[1] Hence the English word 'paradise'

33

Abdalonymos, the leading figure of the hunt, is on horseback and armed with a spear. The master sculptor has given the Sidonian ruler more prominence by placing him in front of Alexander. His combat with the lion forms the central element of the frieze. As was customary for an Oriental ruler of that time, he wears Persian attire.

The use of horses or chariots in lion hunts is known to be an Oriental tradition; this is well documented in Assyrian hunt reliefs from the royal palaces of Nineveh and Nimrud.

Gripping the reins of his charger with the left hand Abdalonymos raises the other up and backwards, to transfix the beast. His hair was ochre yellow; lips and eyes, with pupils in darker tone, were red brown. The colour of his tiara, which was tied by a burgundy ribbon, is indistinguishable, but its flap at the back was red. His tunic was purple with sleeves in burgundy. The anaxyrides was in purple and reddish tones; the shoes probably blue with brown soles. His purple kandys had yellow sleeves lined in blue.

One of the horse's ears is missing. The ribbons which held its forelock and tail were red brown or burgundy. Its girth was red brown and the saddle cloth which was probably an animal skin, had thick red brown fringes.

Although its body is pierced at several points, the lion has stuck its claws into the shoulders of the horse and has torn off a chunk of flesh and gashed its sides; blood was also depicted on the left paw and the shoulder and flank wounds, but not on the thigh wound. Originally, the lion's body had a metal arrow buried in its shoulder and thigh and a lance or javelin in its flank. The horse is sculpted in a classical pose and rather indifferent to what is going on. The lion's form, however, head fully frontal, the upper body turning forward, the rest in profile, perhaps reflects a different tradition. In some respects it bears a resemblance to the lions in combat with rulers on the much earlier Assyrian reliefs.

Behind the lion, a Sidonian in bichrome Persian dress of yellow and blue, has raised his hunting axe with both hands and is about to give a formidable blow to the beast. The wooden handle of his axe was yellow with its iron blade blue.

To the lion's right is another mounted figure in a symmetrical pose. He wears an under tunic, a short-sleeved tunic and a chlamys falling down his back, with corners ending in the shape of a rhombus. His horse has reared up off the ground and its forelegs touch the lion's back. Its rider, who holds the reins with his left hand, has raised his lance to strike the beast. This is thought to be Hephaistion or Krateros, who saved the life of Alexander during a lion hunt at Sidon in 332 BC, when the king was unhorsed. He is probably dressed in an under tunic and chlamys. His left shoe was burgundy and the other brown. His lance was ochre yellow and saddle perhaps yellow, with a fringed saddle cloth. Under his horse, a greyhound bites the lion's left leg.

At the far a right of the main composition is another hunting scene, in which a Greek and a Persian kill a deer. The terrified animal runs to the right, its bleeding wounds indicated in red. The eyes and horns were probably painted black and two metal arrows were buried in its thigh and right shoulder.

The Greek wears a flowing chlamys, fastened on his chest, his body naked. His hair was ochre brown; eyebrows, eyes and lips, red brown. Pulling the horns, he wrenches the deer's head backwards and is about to bury a javelin in its flank. Traces of his purple chlamys with a yellow lower border are barely distinguishable and show that he was probably a 'Personal Companion' of Alexander, one of the elite group of close and noble friends. The purple colour may be a mark of his rank. The distinction attributed to the colour was already established by the reign of Alexander.

On the other side, a hunter in Persian dress raises his axe with both hands to strike the animal; he is in an identical pose with the Oriental behind the lion. His hair was ochre brown; eyebrows, eyes — with darker pupils — and lips were red brown. His tiara was ochre yellow. The tunic was blue with its lower border and sleeves probably burgundy. His anaxyrides bears traces of yellow and a band in burgundy. His kandys was yellow, its blue sleeves filling the background.[2] The garment had a lining in yellow. The handle of the axe was in yellow and its iron blade blue.

It is clear that this composition was intended to show that Abdalonymos, like the rest of the Oriental monarchs, was fond of the royal sport, and partici-pated in lion hunts, accompanied by the greatest of all kings, Alexander the Great.

This hunting scene which brings the Greeks and Persians together can per-haps be interpreted as a symbolic representation of Alexander's conquest of Persia. He seems to have wanted to assimilate the Hellenic and Oriental worlds and create a Graeco-Persian empire. Towards the end of his life he married Oriental princesses, wore Persian dress, and adopted the pomp and protocol of the Persian court. He is even said to have asked his friends to prostrate themselves in front of him in the Oriental manner.

[2] Since this side has less figures than the other long face the sculptor has utilized flowing garments to fill the empty background and thus animate the cold marble surface.

SHORT SIDE A

On one of the shorter sides of the chest is a representation of battle showing three isolated fighting scenes of equal importance. A single-unit effect seems to have been sought by using the same type of shield, showing them at different angles while held in various attitudes. It has been claimed that the mounted Oriental is probably Abdalonymos himself at the battle of Gaza (312 BC), in which he is thought to have been killed.

After the death of Alexander a series of complicated wars began between his generals or Successors (*Diadochi*). Sidon, like the rest of the vassal kingdoms, was unable to isolate itself from these events, where Orientals fought with each other or with Greeks, as did Greeks with one another. It is thought that the battle of Gaza in which Abdalonymos was perhaps killed, took place in late 312 BC. The protagonists were Demetrius, son of Antigonos Monophthalmos (One-Eyed) against Ptolemy of Egypt and Seleucus who later founded his own kingdom in Syria and Mesopotamia.

By this date Antigonos had become Ptolemy's most serious rival, claiming the empire of Alexander for himself. The battle ended with the defeat of Demetrius on whose side Abdalonymos had fought.

In the first combat scene on the left, a Greek soldier attacks his enemy with a metal sword. The Persian retreats and tries to defend himself with his sword, held in his right hand. Both have circular shields like the others in this composition. The traces on the inner face of the Persian's shield show that it was decorated in extraordinary detail with a scene of the Persian royal tent. The wooden shafts which held the tent were rendered as yellow vertical lines; at the top of the canopy they supported was a winged disc.

In this scene, a popular subject of the Persian artistic repertory, the king was seated on a throne with carved legs. Shown in profile and turning right, he was bearded and wearing a tiara. His legs were covered with a piece of white cloth and his raised right hand rested on a sceptre. Behind him stood a servant dressed in a tunic, holding a fly-swat in his left hand and a napkin in the other. In front of the king stood another figure dressed in white anaxyrides and a tunic of the same colour with blue fringes. He was in *proskynesis*, or 'veneration' bent forward respectfully.

The Greek soldier wears a red or purple-coloured long-sleeved tunic or an *exomis* which has left his body naked. Originally the plumes of his Phrygian helmet were metal accessories. The gilt spine of the helmet was applied in colour. The central medallion of his circular shield bore the figure of a woman in profile turned to the left side, probably a goddess. Its rim was painted in yellow.

The central part shows a mounted Persian about to push his lance at a naked Greek fallen on the ground. The rider is in a similar pose to the other figures on the sarcophagus. He holds the reins of his animal with his left hand and with his raised right hand holds a metal lance. The tail of his charger is fastened with a flowing piece of ribbon. His belt buckle was originally metal. It is thought that this rider represents Abdalonymos.

The fallen Greek is weaponless; traces of his broken lance and helmet, originally indicated in colour, survive. He probably bore only an *ephaptis* rendered in colour. Making a last effort to defend himself with his shield, his muscled body rests on one arm, whilst he reaches upwards with the other.

The last combat represents a Greek killing a Persian. His *ephaptis* flows over his left shoulder, its purple colour indicating that he is an officer or a senior soldier. On his Phrygian helmet were metal side plumes. With his left arm, which bears a shield, he violently pulls back the head of his enemy and with the other, stabs his shoulder with a dagger. The Persian falls to his knees. Traces of his tiara, which must have fallen during the struggle, and indicated in yellow paint, survive on the marble surface below his right arm. While his left arm, which bears his shield, is raised helplessly, with his right hand he struggles against the enemy, holding him by the arm.

PEDIMENT A

The pediments of the lid also show fighting scenes. These reliefs compared to those on the casket are of poor workmanship, and must have been executed by less skillful craftsmen, or in haste.

The pediment on this side of the lid shows a skirmish or an ambush scene, which is interpreted as being related to the wars of the Successors. All the combatants are Greeks, probably one group raiding the camp of another. The scene is thought to represent the murder of Perdiccas by Greek soldiers in 320 BC.

In the left angle of the tympanum, a Greek dressed only in a tunic helps his wounded comrade, trying not to attract any attention from the others. He is probably a young Greek servant. His ankle-boots which were indicated in paint are not of the military type. The wounded soldier, armed like those at the centre, wears a metalic cuirass over a short-sleeved tunic. The purple colour of the garment shows that he is from an elite battalion. His red-coloured shield bore a figure.

The similarly armoured soldier who advances from the left has a richly coloured cuirass which is not the standard type. Its breastplate was decorated with a head of Medusa. His lower torso is protected by a kilt of leather strips. The crest of his Phrygian helmet is obscured by the lintel of the pediment. He has taken a step forward in the direction of his adversary and his left foot rests on a rectangular piece of stone. He covers himself with his round shield and in his right hand is a metal sword.

At the centre, a young man is on his knees, his lance on the ground, indicated in colour. A soldier in a cuirass worn over a short-sleeved tunic, with a circular shield on his left shoulder, pulls back the young man's head by his hair and stabs him in the shoulder. Probably an officer, his feet apart, he stands on the left foot of the fallen man. His silver greaves are lined with red garters. His helmet has a gilt spine along the crest, and side plumes. The dying man, draped in a tunic fastened at the left shoulder, has turned his eyes as if begging for mercy, and with both hands holds his assailant's arms. He is dressed in a red *exomis* tunic which leaves his right shoulder free. This was the normal garment worn by the Greek mercenaries — who also did not wear cuirasses, or bear arms. This confirms the idea of an ambush.

49

The figure is thought to represent Perdiccas. However, his murderer has already turned his attention to the enemy who rushes to the rescue of his fallen friend. After the death of Alexander, his general Perdiccas became the regent for both Philip III, Arrhidaios, the weak-minded son of Philip II, and Alexander IV, the child of Alexander by his Sogdian wife Roxane. In 320 BC Perdiccas tried to cross the Nile and invade Egypt, but was killed in his tent by his own officers who had changed sides and joined with Ptolemy I of Egypt.

Ancient sources are silent about the effect of Perdiccas's death on the fortunes of Abdalonymos. Nevertheless, he is assumed to have kept his throne both during the reign of Antigonus Monophthalmos, who became regent for Alexander's son and half-brother, and during Ptolemy's brief occupation of Phoenicia. These events took place around 312 BC, perhaps the period when the sarcophagus was made.

To the right, a Greek — thought to represent Alexander's half-brother Philip — covers himself with his shield and drives his lance into an enemy, who is already wounded and on his knees. He wears a muscle cuirass which reflects the shape of his physique and no helmet, but a narrow headband. His laced-boots are indicated in paint and his right foot is on a piece of stone. He is the only bearded Greek on the sarcophagus, the others all being clean-shaven. Although Alexander wanted his soldiers not to grow beards — to deny the enemy a hand-hold during close combat — some officers did not give up the ancient tradition. In the background, a helmet, probably his, and a lance which must have belonged to his enemy, are shown in paint. The final figure is badly damaged, but gives the impression that he was naked. Almost nothing survives from the last figure who was placed in the angle on this side.

The pediment is surmounted with an acroterion in the shape of a double palmette springing from an acanthus motif flanked by two Persian griffons placed symmetrically.

SHORT SIDE B

On this short side of the chest a panther hunt is depicted. All of the five participants are Sidonians dressed in the Persian manner. By the absence of Greeks from this relief the artist may have wanted to show that the royal hunt was a part of the normal life of Sidonian nobility even before the arrival of the Greeks.

On the left a groom tries to control the scared horse of his master. His anaxyrides is decorated with slightly incised vertical ovals. The bit and bridle of the animal were metal; the groom probably held a piece of the latter in his right hand. The left hoof and left ear of the animal have not survived. It had a red saddle which was decorated with two horned and winged griffons in white and advancing left. Behind the groom and horse, a greyhound runs towards the panther.

At the centre, the master of the hunt aims a metal javelin at the panther, which is shown in profile. His left arm bears a circular shield whose armgrip was indicated in ochre yellow paint. The shield's interior was decorated with a disc in blue and surrounded by two circles, the outer one jagged. There was also a ring of nails forming a relief decoration. The rim had a band of egg and tongue in yellow, filled with red brown. He is dressed in the Persian manner and wears blue shoes. He may represent Abdalonymos. According to Xenophon, for the Persians the shield was a part of the hunting gear.

The panther is shown with the conventional features of the period. Its head is very small for its long neck. Its paws are too long. The forequarters of the body are also too big and the hindquarters too small. It is shown in an indecisive stage of action. While its left paw rests on the ground, its other is raised as if to strike. The eyes were probably indicated in yellow paint. Blood was dripping from its wounds. From the other side three grooms attack the panther.

The first of these is a figure with a red moustache. His bichrome anaxyrides was painted in red brown, yellow or blue. With both hands he has raised a hunting axe and is about to hit the beast. The handle of the axe was yellow and its iron blade blue.

The second groom has thrust his lance into the back of the panther, from which blood gushed. The yellow paint of the lance's shaft can be seen above his right hand. His hair, eyes — with the pupils shown darker — and moustache were red brown. His tiara bears traces of yellow paint. His tunic was red with its sleeves ending in blue at the wrist. The lower border of the garment was burgundy. His anaxyrides was blue and his shoes yellow.

The third figure, whose left arm has not survived, has also driven his metal lance into the animal.

PEDIMENT B

The pediment on this side shows a fight between the Persians and the Greeks. The scene is interpreted as showing the soldiers of Abdalonymos fighting Greeks. In the angle of the tympanum a dead Greek soldier is seen — dressed in a red tunic and wearing yellow cuirass — on the ground. His shoes were red with black laces. In the background a broken lance was painted in yellow brown.

To the right of this is a Persian with one knee bent to the ground. He is draped in a long-sleeved tunic held with a single belt. His right arm which carried a metal sword is drawn back to strike. On his left arm he carries a pelta which was decorated with a blue winged and yellow headed figure on a purple background. Its border was painted in yellow brown. Its was held by a red armgrip. He wears standard cavalry boots.

The third figure is a Greek soldier who stands with his legs wide apart. His shoes are of the same type as those of the figure behind him. He wears a red tunic under purple armour; the shoulder straps of his cuirass were also in purple. He was armed with a metal sword in his right hand and with a small shield held in the other. In the background his fallen lance and broken helmet were indicated in colour, lying behind the figure on the ground. The pieces may have been the shafts of his lance and that of another fighter. His helmet was decorated with two double-volutes around the casque and plumes on either side, all rendered in yellow paint. Among all the figures in the reliefs of the sarcophagus this is the only one which shows hasty workmanship and this only on the head and hair.

At the centre of the composition is a mounted figure in Persian costume shown in left profile, his metal lance raised in a threatening attitude; he is tentatively identified as Abdalonymos. He wears armour but no helmet and his furred kandys flows at his back. Originally the latter was speckled like a leopardskin. His saddle was decorated with a stylized foliage pattern. Its border was red and terminated with a blue fringe and black contour lines.

On the opposite side of the pediment another Persian covers himself with his pelta while attacking a Greek with his metal lance. In addition to his usual Persian style costume he wears armour. His cuirass was yellow to represent metal and its breastplate might have had a yellow Medusa decorating the purple stripe at the centre. The border of his shield was ochre brown and its centre purple. It was decorated with two fighting figures shown in yellow. Its armgrip was blue. His anaxyrides was decorated with stripes. The red brown traces behind his right leg may have belonged to an object or perhaps to the undulating terrain.

The last figure has tucked himself behind his shield waiting for a chance to run his enemy through with the sword held in his right hand. He wears only a tunic or *exomis* which leaves his right shoulder open. His face is turned to the left and not visible. The top of his helmet is obscured by the frame of the pediment. The central medallion of his shield was in deep purple colour. His boots are similar to the type worn by the cavalry. He may have been a hypastist.[1] In the angle of the tympanum are a shield and a conical Greek helmet of Phrygian type with a crest and a lance. Among the reliefs of the sarcophagus, the figures and the composition of this pediment are the least interesting.

The pediment is topped with an acroterion in the shape of a large motif of double palmettes springing from an acanthus piece flanked by two Persian griffons placed symmetrically.

[1] In Greek *Hypastistes* means 'shield-bearer': in Alexander's army a regiment whose leaders were trusted with carrying the king's personal weapons

STYLE AND ORNAMENTATION

The sarcophagus,[1] which has dimensions of 195 x 318 x 167 cm, consists of three separate elements. At the base there is an undecorated plinth. Resting on this is the rectangular chest with decorative mouldings above and beneath its framed relief panels. This is surmounted by a deep lid in the form of a Greek temple roof. The combination of shape, proportions and architectural ornament, conveys an impression not only of a sumptuous house of eternity, but almost of a temple in miniature.

Indeed, there were precedents for burial in a sarcophagus like a temple, a famous example being the Nereid Tomb from Xanthos (*c* 400), in the form of a small Ionic temple. Although the practice of inhumation in a sarcophagus, effectively a chest, of stone or wood, was very ancient, the use of elaborately carved sarcophagi developed in Asia Minor, Cyprus, Phoenica and environs in the fifth and fourth centuries BC. Their prototypes, such as that already mentioned and the Mausoleum from Halicarnassus,[2] were made by Greek sculptors, who adapted their knowledge and skills to the taste of the Oriental rulers for whom they worked.

In the course of time, the colossal size of these monumental tombs diminished and their shapes, which were inspired by structures in Asia, were re-

[1] The ancient Greeks held that a realm of darkness was occupied by demons and such like who were believed to be *sarcophageo,* or 'flesh eaters' of the buried. Later the epithet was transferred to a kind of limestone quarried near Assos and to the coffins which were made of this stone. Thus the coffins (*sarcophagi*) are thought to cause the disintegration of the flesh of bodies deposited in them.

[2] Both are restored and displayed in the British Museum.

placed by purely Greek types; i.e. with their lids taking the shape and size of Classical roofs with triangular pediments and acroteria, the decoration on their caskets being rendered between columns or in the form of unbroken friezes.

Beneath the chest's framed relief are two ornate mouldings, separated by an unornamented concave moulding with listels. The torus of the wider and slightly deeper base moulding is decorated with interlaced guilloche bands, as is the narrower torus of the upper moulding, where the decoration runs in the opposite direction. Above this, separated by a listel, is a band of stylized lotus flowers and palmettes and finally, a narrow band of bead and reel. There are palmettes at the corners.

Above the relief, a narrower moulding repeats the bead and reel, followed by a band of egg and tongue, with inverted palmettes at the corners. There is then a thick border of double meander, with plain bands at the upper and lower edges.

The precision with which the mouldings were carved suggests a confident familiarity with Classical Greek ornamentation, though in its lavish use, albeit to splendid effect, Classical norms of restraint have been abandoned. So too, was there familiarity with the repertory of Eastern royal and funerary symbolism, the latter particularly evident in the decoration of the lid.

There is a badly damaged band of bead and reel at the base of the lid, above which is a thin band of lotus flowers and palmettes. An unadorned concave moulding separates this from a scroll of vine leaves worked in low relief. To emphasize their shape, each leaf was drilled to create indentations, but not always accurately, so that many have four small holes, instead of the well defined curves of this distinctive leaf. The background was originally wine coloured and the leaves autumnal yellow; the fruit harvested, the dying leaves of the approaching winter reinforce the symbolism of death. The cornice above consists of a band of dentils and another of egg and tongue.

On the long sides projecting above the cornice, are twelve gargoyle griffons

60

in imitation of gutters, each with an animal muzzle and three horns curling backwards. Originally, the contour lines of the eyes, muzzles and the depression below the central horn were painted in red brown.

Above and set between the griffons, are nine goddess heads forming the antefux, as on a roof. Each has a diadem enveloped in a crown of open leaves and rosettes on either side of the neck. They are thought to represent the goddess Atargatis, who symbolized death in winter and birth in spring and was the Syrian counterpart of the Great Mother Goddess of Anatolian and Mesopotamian cultures, worshipped since prehistoric times. Adorning the corners are four superbly worked recumbent and snarling lions, guardians of the tomb, and a common motif in Ionian art.

The ridge-pole of the acroterion is decorated with female heads like those above the projection, but in the form of double sided masks with wings on either side of their necks. Between these were eagles, which have not survived, but for some restored pieces of their wings. In Syria the bird was the symbol of the sky god Hadad, later syncretised with Zeus and also the bird which carried the souls of the dead to heaven. This suggests that the masks could perhaps represent the sirens who also carried the souls of the dead to heaven. This was a popular motif of Greek funerary iconography widely utilized elsewhere.

At each end, above the pediments, the acroteria terminates in a double palmette springing from an acanthus, flanked by two Persian griffons. These have the slender bodies of dogs, small muzzles, thin necks and their wings furled back in the archaic fashion.

In many respects, as the use of all the various decorative and figural traditions shows, this sarcophagus, one of the finest specimens of its type, represents a convergence of different worlds and traditions.

Scholars think that it is the work of more than a single sculptor. One of the master sculptors thought to have executed it was probably somebody who worked in Attica and was influenced by the painting style of Philoxenus of Eretria, the painter of the battle scene — of either Issos or Gaugamela — for Kassandros, a general of Alexander who later became king of Macedon (317-307 BC). The Alexander mosaic which was discovered at the House of the Faun in Pompei[3] (c. 150 BC) is thought to have been inspired by this mural. The influence of Philoxenus shows itself mostly in the combat scenes such as that of the Persian soldier being killed by Alexander as his horse falls on its forelegs, or the accumulation of fight at the centre of the compositon, both characteristics displayed on the long face A.

The heroic nudity of some of the Macedonian figures confirms the Classical Greek funerary sculpture. This applies also to their calm faces and relaxed movements. Their enemies are often depicted with realistic and more natural physiognomy and agitated movements foreshadowing the Hellenistic rendering often accorded to barbarians or slaves.

The second master sculptor(s) obviously preferred the East-Greek tradition and his their work displays itself in the panther and lion hunt representations. It is certain that the first sculptor allowed a certain amount of freedom to the second.

There is no information about the identity of the sculptor(s). However, it is unlikely that a famous sculptor would have accepted a commission where his work would end in an underground burial chamber.

The painters of the sarcophagus appear to have been as skillful as the sculptor(s). Originally, the hair, eyes, eyelashes, lips and clothing of the figures were painted in tones of yellow, burnt sienna, blue, red and purple, while the flesh area was given only a slight lacquer. However, only traces were left from its paint when it was discovered.

[3] Now in the National Museum of Naples

SELECTED BIBLIOGRAPHY

Pasinli, A., *İstanbul Archaeological Museum*, İstanbul, 1996 pp. 85-101,

Pasinli, A., Les Musèe Archéologiques d'İstanbul, İstanbul, 1989, pp. 18-33

Sekunda, N., *The Army of Alexander the Great*, London, 1984

Lipsius, F., *Alexander the Great,* London, 1974

Mansel, A.M., Graeve, von V., 'Der Alexandersarkophag und seine Werkstatt' *Belleten* 36, 1972, s. 99-106

Graeve, von V., 'Der Alexandersarkophag und seine Werkstatt', *Ist. Forsch.* 28, 1970

Schefold, K., Seidel, M., *Der Alexander Sarkophag,* Berlin, 1968

Kleiner, G., *Diadochengraeber*, Wiesbaden, 1963

Kleemann, I., 'Der Satrapensarkophag aus Sidon', *Ist Forsch.* 20, 1958

Mendel, G., *Catalogue des sculptures grecques, romaines et byzantines (Musee Impériaux Ottomans),* Vol I, Constantinople, 1912, pp. 171-200

Winter, F., *Der Alexandersarkophag aus Sidon,* Strassburg, 1912

Willrich, H., 'Krateros und der Grabherr des Alexandersarkophags von Sidon', *Hermes 34,* 1899 p. 231 ff.

Studniczka, F., 'Über die Grundlagen der geschichtlichen Erklarung der sidonischen Sarkophage', *Jdl. 9,* 1894, pp. 204-244

Winter, F., *'Die Sarkophages von Sidon'* AA I, 1894, s.1-23

Judeich, W., 'Der Grabherr des 'Alexandersarkophags' ' *Jdl. 10,* 1895, pp. 165-182

Hamdi, O. Reinach, Th., *Une Nécropole Royale à Sidon,* Paris, 1892